BRODSWORTH HALL AND GARDENS

CAROLINE CARR-WHITWORTH
Historic Properties, English Heritage

BRODSWORTH HALL *with its garden was given to English Heritage in 1990 by Mrs Pamela Williams. The contents of the house were purchased by the National Heritage Memorial Fund for £3.36 million and transferred to English Heritage. During the following five years, before opening to the public in 1995, the property underwent a major programme of restoration and conservation.*

Brodsworth is an outstanding example of a Victorian country house. It was built and furnished in only three years between 1861 and 1863, and has survived with most of its original contents. However, by 1990 the house and contents were in a perilous state of decay; mining subsidence, water penetration and eroding stonework had caused serious damage to the building, and this has been extensively repaired. The overgrown gardens have also been much restored. By contrast the interior, where successive generations have all left their mark on the original Victorian scheme, has been conserved largely as it was found rather than restored. The decoration and contents had suffered from the ravages of time, light, damp, dust and insect infestation, and

extensi[...] has bee[...] preserve[...]

The Brodsworth estate and its mid-eighteenth-century house were acquired by Peter Thellusson, a banker, in about 1790. In an extra-ordinary will, he left it and the rest of his fortune to accumulate for three generations. It was eventually inherited by Charles Sabine Augustus Thellusson, who decided to demolish the house and build anew in the 1860s. His new house, the present Brodsworth Hall, incorporates many fixtures such as chimneypieces and doors from the earlier house. The interiors were largely furnished by the London firm of Lapworths, though earlier furnishings were also reused and subsequent generations of the family have both redecorated many rooms and added to the collections.

In 1931 the estate was inherited by Charles Sabine's grandson, Charles Grant-Dalton. It was his daughter, Pamela Williams, who after her mother's death in 1988 gave the house and gardens to English Heritage. Sadly she died in 1994, and thus did not live to see the start of a new era in the house's history.

ABOVE *'Prairie Prince', one of the family pets, painted in 1897. His name is inscribed on the book and the letter is addressed to 'Thellusson, Brodsworth Hall'*

The Thellusson family has had a long and distinguished history. They were Huguenot (Protestant) landowners in the Lyons area of France, and fled to Switzerland to escape religious persecution in the mid-sixteenth century.

The family always showed great financial acumen. Theophile Thellusson (1646–1705) established a financial business, which his son Isaac effectively turned into a bank, 'Thellusson et Companie'. Isaac's career flourished; he was the Genevan ambassador at Paris from 1730, visiting Louis XV at Versailles and receiving many honours. On his death in 1755 he left a considerable fortune, including many works of art.

Isaac Thellusson's sons also had successful financial careers; in 1753 Georges-Tobie formed the bank 'Thellusson, Necker et Companie'.

Sarah, Madame Isaac Thellusson, painted by Nicolas de Largillière in 1725. Her son Peter made the famous will which eventually enabled Brodsworth to be built

Peter Thellusson (1735–97)

Isaac's youngest son, Peter, came to London in about 1760. He acted as agent for his brother before establishing his own banking business at Philpot Lane in the City. In 1761 he became a British citizen and in the same year married Anne Woodford, from a Lincolnshire landowning family. He bought the extensive Brodsworth estates in Yorkshire and was buried there in 1797.

The eighteenth-century Brodsworth Hall, bought by Peter Thellusson. The photograph was taken in about 1850 before the house was demolished to make way for the present hall

The famous will

Peter Thellusson amassed a huge fortune. At his death it was estimated at around £700,000, or approximately £34 million at today's prices. The terms of his will were unusual and caused an immediate sensation, with his family contesting it in the courts. It has been famous ever since.

After bequests to his family of about £100,000, the remainder of Peter Thellusson's fortune was to be left in trust to accumulate during the lives of any of his sons, grandsons and great-grandsons who were alive at his death. On the death of the last of these, the estate would be divided between 'the eldest male lineal descendents of my three sons then living'. If there were no such descendents, it was to be used to help pay off the National Debt! There was widespread concern that fortunes of this size, accumulated for so long and concentrated in the hands of a few individuals, might be so vast as to disturb the economy of the whole country – 'an object impolitic and pernicious', according to his family's lawyers.

Thellusson's immediate family disputed the will in court soon after his death, but in spite of severe criticism it was upheld. Because of the serious issues involved, in 1800 Parliament passed the Accumulations Act, often called the Thellusson Act, which limited the length of time that property could be left to accumulate.

At the time of Peter Thellusson's death, nine of his sons and grandsons were alive. With the death in 1856 of the last of them – his grandson Charles – the long period governed by the will eventually came to an end. The final court judgement declared that the inheritance should be shared by two people, Frederick, the fourth Lord Rendlesham, and Charles Sabine Augustus Thellusson. It has been said that the amount of money they eventually inherited was not substantially greater than that originally left, largely owing to the expense of all the litigation which continued long after Thellusson's death. There are parallels with the case of Jarndyce *v.* Jarndyce in Charles Dickens's *Bleak House*: Dickens himself said his novel reflected various celebrated cases of the day.

FAMILY TREE OF THE
THELLUSSON AND GRANT-DALTON FAMILIES

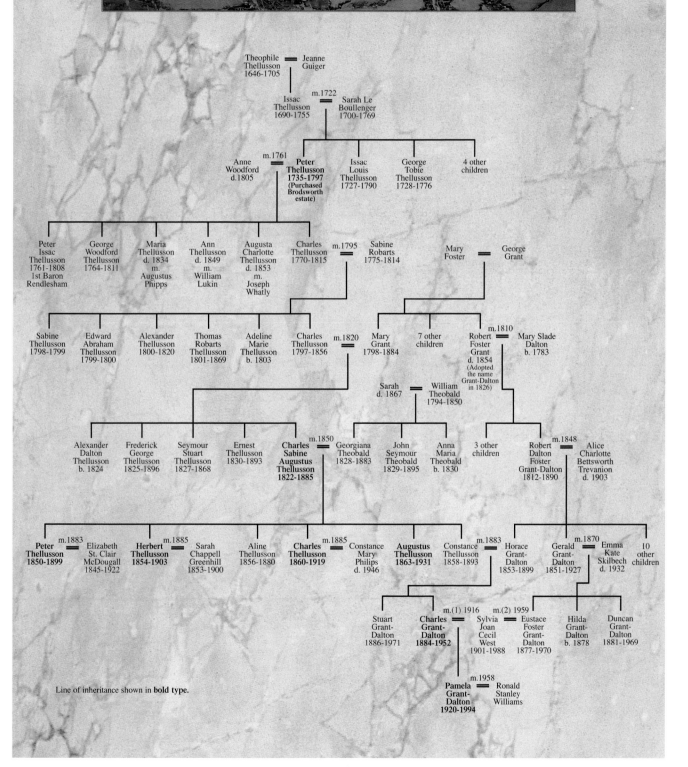

Theophile Thellusson 1646-1705 **═** Jeanne Guiger

m.1722

Issac Thellusson 1690-1755 **═══** Sarah Le Boullenger 1700-1769

Anne Woodford d.1805 **═** m.1761 **Peter Thellusson 1735-1797 (Purchased Brodsworth estate)**

Issac Louis Thellusson 1727-1790

George Tobie Thellusson 1728-1776

4 other children

Peter Issac Thellusson 1761-1808 1st Baron Rendlesham

George Woodford Thellusson 1764-1811

Maria Thellusson d. 1834 m. Augustus Phipps

Ann Thellusson d. 1849 m. William Lukin

Augusta Charlotte Thellusson d. 1853 m. Joseph Whatly

Charles Thellusson 1770-1815 **═** m.1795 Sabine Robarts 1775-1814

Mary Foster **═══** George Grant

Sabine Thellusson 1798-1799

Edward Abraham Thellusson 1799-1800

Alexander Thellusson 1800-1820

Thomas Robarts Thellusson 1801-1869

Adeline Marie Thellusson b. 1803

Charles Thellusson 1797-1856 **═** m.1820

Mary Grant 1798-1884

7 other children

Robert Foster Grant d. 1854 (Adopted the name Grant-Dalton in 1826) **═** m.1810 Mary Slade Dalton b. 1783

Sarah d. 1867 **═══** William Theobald 1794-1850

Alexander Dalton Thellusson b. 1824

Frederick George Thellusson 1825-1896

Seymour Stuart Thellusson 1827-1868

Ernest Thellusson 1830-1893

Charles Sabine Augustus Thellusson 1822-1885 **═** m.1850

Georgiana Theobald 1828-1883

John Seymour Theobald 1829-1895

Anna Maria Theobald b. 1830

3 other children

Robert Dalton Foster Grant-Dalton 1812-1890 **═** m.1848 Alice Charlotte Bettsworth Trevanion d. 1903

Peter Thellusson 1850-1899 **═** m.1883 Elizabeth St. Clair McDougall 1845-1922

Herbert Thellusson 1854-1903 **═** m.1885 Sarah Chappell Greenhill 1853-1900

Aline Thellusson 1856-1880

Charles Thellusson 1860-1919 **═** m.1885 Constance Mary Philips d. 1946

Augustus Thellusson 1863-1931

Constance Thellusson 1858-1893 **═** m.1883

Horace Grant-Dalton 1853-1899

Gerald Grant-Dalton 1851-1927 **═** m.1870 Emma Kate Skilbech d. 1932

10 other children

Stuart Grant-Dalton 1886-1971

Charles Grant-Dalton 1884-1952 **═** m.(1) 1916

Sylvia Joan Cecil West 1901-1988 **═** m.(2) 1959 Eustace Foster Grant-Dalton 1877-1970

Hilda Grant-Dalton b. 1878

Duncan Grant-Dalton 1881-1969

Pamela Grant-Dalton 1920-1994 **═** m.1958 Ronald Stanley Williams

Line of inheritance shown in **bold type**.

Charles Thellusson commissioned this large portrait by the fashionable artist Sir Thomas Lawrence of his wife Sabine and eldest son Charles in 1804. It was the death in 1856 of Charles, the boy in the painting, which released the fortune left in his grandfather's will

Peter Thellusson has been accused of miserliness towards his immediate family. However, he did not entirely disinherit them, and they all received substantial bequests by the values of the time. His children prospered, his three daughters making good marriages. His eldest son Peter was made an Irish peer, the first Baron Rendlesham, and the two younger sons, George and Charles, both became MPs.

Charles (1770–1815) seems to have lived at Brodsworth towards the end of his life, and died there in 1815. He was married to Sabine Robarts, the daughter of a banker, and they had six children.

Charles Thellusson (1797–1856)

The eldest of the six children of Charles and Sabine Thellusson, also called Charles, seems to have spent much of his early life abroad, and in 1820 married Mary Grant in Paris. This was the start of a long connection between the Thellusson, Grant and Grant-Dalton families. By 1849 he and his family had returned to England and settled at 'The Casino', Worthing.

Charles's diaries reveal that he was often beset by debts. He lived a sociable life, dining out, playing billiards and attending race meetings. By 1854 he seems to have become the part-owner of Rataplan, a celebrated racehorse from the stud of his daughter-in-law's family, which

clearly brought him some useful income. His diary for that year gleefully records that 'Up to this time … I calculate Rataplan has won 13 races out of 17, about £3238 after deducting stake.' He also estimates how much his son might inherit from the famous will on his own death.

Charles Sabine Augustus Thellusson (1822–85)

The eldest of Charles Thellusson's five children, Charles Sabine, was born in Florence and later became a captain in the 12th Lancers. In 1850 he married Georgiana Theobald, whose grandfather, John Theobald, had built up a successful stud of racehorses after making his fortune in the hosiery trade.

Charles Sabine must have grown up with the knowledge that he would be one of his great-grandfather's heirs. In 1859 he finally came into his half-share of the fortune, which included the Brodsworth estate. At that time Charles was living in Brighton with a growing family, and he rapidly decided to rebuild Brodsworth Hall as a more comfortable and up-to-date family house. By the end of the 1860s the new household was fully established with a staff of fifteen indoor servants, including a butler, housekeeper, cook, nurse, three footmen and various maids. This was the only time that Brodsworth housed a large family of children.

Charles Sabine Augustus Thellusson's innovative and prize-winning yacht the Aline, *launched in 1860*

Before coming into his inheritance Charles Sabine had developed an interest in yachting, which became his and his family's main enthusiasm. The four major sailing yachts he commissioned between 1854 and 1874 – *Georgiana, Aline, Guinevere* and *Bodicea* – had a profound influence on British yacht design, the last two being successively the largest yachts in the world.

This painting of the famous racehorse Rataplan in 1851 by Harry Hall hangs with several other equestrian paintings in the Billiard Room

LEFT *A watercolour of the south front of Brodsworth Hall, possibly by the architect Philip Wilkinson in about 1861, showing only minor differences from the house as it was built*

INSET *Charles Sabine Augustus Thellusson, the builder of Brodsworth Hall, photographed in 1878*

Constance Thellusson with her copy of The Music Lesson, *one of her father's Dutch paintings which used to hang in the Dining Room*

The family also enjoyed artistic pursuits. Music was provided by a grand piano in the Drawing Room, and there was an organ in the South Hall. Charles's children Herbert and Aline produced watercolours and oil paintings, some of which hang in the house.

The family's fondness for pets is evident both in paintings and in the 'pets' cemetery' with its inscribed headstones in the garden.

After Charles Sabine's death in 1885, Brodsworth Hall was inherited by each of his sons in turn. Since none of them had any children, however, it eventually passed to their sister Constance's eldest son, Charles Grant-Dalton, in 1931.

Charles Sabine's children

PETER THELLUSSON (1850–99)

Charles Sabine's eldest son, Peter, was educated at Oxford and had scholarly interests; he bought many books for the Library. He was also a keen photographer, recording his family, yachts and travels abroad. In 1883 he married Elizabeth McDougall, who had come to Brodsworth as a 'Companion', either for his mother or his sister Constance. Although he had no children, Peter

maintained as large a household staff as his father had. He also undertook a series of costly repairs to both the house and estate buildings, including some redecoration.

HERBERT THELLUSSON (1854–1903)

Charles Sabine's second son, Herbert, and his wife Sarah hardly lived at Brodsworth long enough to effect any changes. However, much of the extensive collection of household linen at Brodsworth bears his monogram.

CHARLES THELLUSSON (1860–1919)

Charles, the third son of Charles Sabine, married Constance Mary Philips, the daughter of the local rector, in 1885. They lived at Brodsworth from 1903 to 1919, during which time the house and estate flourished. Charles permitted the newly formed Brodsworth Colliery Company to extract coal from under the estate. He also rented the company land to build Woodlands, a model miners' village, for which he funded the erection of the church, the spire of which can still be seen aligned on Brodsworth Hall's drive. He also built a model farm, breeding prize-winning Jersey and Aberdeen Angus herds.

The six children of Charles Sabine Thellusson, from a family album, in about 1870

On the death in 1931 of the last of Charles Sabine's sons, Brodsworth passed to Charles Grant-Dalton (1884–1952), the elder son of their sister Constance. Charles, who served as a captain with the Royal Army Service Corps in the First World War, had married Sylvia West in 1916. They had one daughter, Pamela, and lived initially at Lymington in Hampshire. They owned a succession of yachts, including the steam yacht *Sylvia*. Charles also loved cars, and owned Rolls-Royces and a Bentley.

Captain Charles Grant-Dalton in an army Rolls-Royce Silver Ghost in about 1915

When the Grant-Daltons first came to live at Brodsworth it must have seemed a daunting prospect. They gradually adapted the large and old-fashioned house to make it easier to run, employing a much smaller staff, and abandoning the huge Victorian kitchen. Sylvia had many of the bedrooms painted in modern colours, and closed up some rooms altogether, while Captain

The opening of the Brodsworth Colliery in 1905, when Charles Thellusson turned the first sod. He is to the left of his wife Constance, who stands behind the ceremonial spade and barrow

George V is reputed to have been interested enough in his schemes to make a royal visit soon after his accession. Another famous occasion was Charles and Constance's silver wedding anniversary, celebrated in 1910 with many gifts, a banquet and 'meat tea' for 500 villagers.

Charles and Constance were responsible for the electrification of the hall in about 1913. They also replaced the original crimson silk wall coverings in the South Hall with the present yellow silk, and carried out extensive redecoration and refurbishment of the bedrooms.

The couple enjoyed entertaining and travelling, and would take to their yacht each year. They had holidays in Norway, Scotland and the Caribbean. They were hospitable to all their many nephews and nieces, by whom Charles was affectionately known as 'Uncle Bill'.

AUGUSTUS THELLUSSON (1863–1931)
After Charles's relatively early death in 1919 his widow returned to their previous home in Torquay, and Brodsworth was inherited by the fourth and youngest of Charles Sabine's sons, Augustus. He never married, but established himself in a comfortable house at Broadstairs in Kent. He seems only to have visited Brodsworth once a year for the shooting, so during the 1920s it was little used and maintained by a very small staff. Augustus is thought to have suffered badly from gout, and may have used the wooden wheelchair at Brodsworth. He had the family liking for pets, owning several dogs and even a pair of marmosets (little monkeys) which are reputed to have lived in the Library.

RIGHT *Sylvia Grant-Dalton with her daughter Pamela in about 1925*

Reminders of the war: a military notice on the back of the Kitchen door with instructions in case of air raids or gas attack, and a gas mask

Grant-Dalton undertook to wind the clocks and clean the Drawing Room chandeliers himself. In spite of the difficulties of running such a large house, the Grant-Daltons often entertained, hosting the local Hunt Ball on more than one occasion.

During the Second World War Brodsworth was requisitioned by the Army. The original Kitchen was brought back into service, while the family kept only the Library and a few bedrooms for their own use. Black-out blinds in the Kitchen and graffiti found on the leadwork of the roof are amongst the reminders of the war at Brodsworth. After the war further alterations were undertaken, such as the introduction of plumbed washbasins in many of the bedrooms, and the installation of a lift for Captain Grant-Dalton.

Some years after Charles's death Sylvia married his cousin, Major Eustace Grant-Dalton, who, as she said, 'got into every war he could', including the Boer War and both world wars. After his death in 1970 Sylvia continued to live at Brodsworth, but this became more and more of a struggle as she grew older. She died in 1988 at the age of 87, having lived at Brodsworth for 56 years.

Sylvia was the force which had kept Brodsworth going, patching it up as best she could but fighting a losing battle against the effects of mining subsidence and a leaking roof. She was keen that the house and its contents should be preserved, and her desire was realised in 1990 when her daughter, Pamela Williams, generously gave Brodsworth Hall and its gardens to English Heritage. The contents were purchased by the National Heritage Memorial

ABOVE LEFT Sylvia Grant-Dalton took an active interest in local affairs and good causes. She and Pamela are photographed here with other Red Cross Volunteers during the Second World War. Sylvia is on the front row, second from the left, and Pamela is second from the right at the back

Fund and transferred to English Heritage. Sadly Mrs Williams died in 1994, before seeing the opening of Brodsworth Hall to the public in the following year.

Pamela Grant-Dalton with one of the marble greyhounds and her own dogs. Greyhounds also feature in the family crest

7

RIGHT *The south front of the present Brodsworth Hall in about 1910. Charles Thellusson, the third son of the builder Charles Sabine, stands on the steps with his wife Constance*

Although Brodsworth Hall was built in a short period of a few years in the mid-nineteenth century, the area has a long history of occupation. The Roman road from Doncaster ran nearby and the village is mentioned in Domesday Book. In 1713 the Brodsworth estate was bought by the seventh Earl of Kinnoul, who is known to have improved an existing house and estate, planting many trees. His younger son, Robert Hay Drummond, later the Archbishop of York, carried out further improvements and lived at Brodsworth in considerable style.

The Brodsworth estate was purchased in about 1790 from the archbishop's son by Peter Thellusson. By the time Charles Sabine Thellusson came into his inheritance in 1859 the house must have seemed old fashioned and cumbersome; he lost no time in using his new fortune to demolish it and build anew.

The substantial size of the eighteenth-century house can be gauged from this photograph taken in the 1850s

Construction

Charles Thellusson's new Brodsworth Hall, the present house, was built and furnished between 1861 and 1863, although further work continued to the house and grounds for the rest of the decade. A good proportion of its original decoration and contents survives, although many changes have been made by later generations. The building and later history of the house are well documented by bills, inventories and photographs: together with the house and contents, these give us a remarkable glimpse of a house of the 1860s which has been lived in until the late twentieth century.

In spite of the wealth of documentation, the architect of Brodsworth remains somewhat mysterious. A little-known London architect, Philip Wilkinson, specified and supervised the building work, undertaken by the London firm Longmire & Burge.

The house is built of soft pale magnesian limestone, some of which was quarried on the Brodsworth estate. Much material from the old house was reused, including stonework, windows and internal fittings. By late 1863 the building work was almost complete, and the house had been supplied with new carpets, curtains and furniture by Lapworth Brothers of London. The total cost, including furnishings, grounds, park and cottages, was just under £50,000.

There continued to be expenditure on laying out the grounds until 1870. Old buildings and hedges were removed, new drives made, trees and shrubs planted, and garden buildings and bridges in 'the Grove' constructed (see page 32). In 1865–66 an Italian architect and sculptor, Chevaliere G. M. Casentini, provided Thellusson with a large number of marble statues and ornaments for the garden.

Architectural style

Brodsworth was built in a restrained Italianate style and to a clear T-shaped plan. The main block is long and low (only two storeys) with an even lower adjoining servants' wing at the back. Each side of the house is strictly symmetrical, with false windows added where they were not needed by the plan of the rooms. Its regularity of form, however, is enlivened by subtle

OPPOSITE *The West Hall seen from the South Hall, with the original carpets and curtains and some of Charles Sabine's sculpture collection*

RIGHT *The Smoking Room in 1910. Originally the School Room, it became a Smoking Room once Charles Sabine's children had grown up. It later fell into disrepair and is not now open to the public*

variations in architectural detail, such as the two slightly projecting bays on the long south front, and the columned 'porte cochère', to shelter those entering the house, on the short east front.

Brodsworth's classical style, the simplicity of its form and the way it sits solidly in its formal gardens is rather unusual for a time when country houses were being designed to fit more picturesquely into their setting. By the 1860s the irregular Gothic or Elizabethan styles were considered more appropriate for the English countryside than symmetrical classicism. Even the Italianate country houses of the 1840s and '50s, most notably Queen Victoria's Osborne House on the Isle of Wight, were usually given diversity by a tower or by the grouping of their elements. In contrast Brodsworth's compact and regular form is very urban, drawing on Italian town palaces and London houses and clubs rather than country villas.

Interior plan and functioning

The interior of Brodsworth Hall is typical of a mid-nineteenth-century country house in plan, function and furnishings. The house was built to accommodate Charles Thellusson and his family of six children, to entertain their guests, and to house a large staff of at least fifteen servants.

The ideas and sense of decorum of the time required that specific rooms and even areas of the house be set aside for different people and activities. The main family rooms, including a Morning Room, Dining Room, Library, Billiard Room and Drawing Rooms, show how the family organised their time and occupations. Some rooms, such as the Billiard Room, were predominantly the men's domain, while the Drawing Rooms were the women's, and this is reflected in their decoration. The children were housed in an area behind the Great Staircase consisting of a School Room, Day and Night Nurseries and Governess's room. Thus, appropriately to their status, they were positioned half way between the servants' quarters and the main family rooms. The servants were housed in the adjoining block at the back, as was

The Drawing Rooms in the 1880s, showing many of the furnishings supplied by Lapworths, including the carpet, wall coverings and chandeliers. Note the chintz curtains and case covers to protect the silk upholstery, and the sculptures placed near the windows

standard practice. The family and servants each had their own staircases, and doors, baize-covered upstairs, kept the two firmly apart.

As the exterior suggests, the interior is arranged on a very regular plan. From the front door a series of halls and corridors leads to the main reception rooms, all of which look out on the gardens to the south and west. This arrangement is repeated on the first floor with all the bedrooms overlooking the garden and connected by a long, wide internal corridor.

The most unusual aspect of Brodsworth's interior is the extravagant proportions of the circulation spaces of halls and corridors, providing a series of impressive spaces and vistas through the house. By comparison the main family rooms and bedrooms, with the exception of the Drawing Rooms, are not excessively large but comfortably proportioned.

Servants and servicing the house

A comprehensive and well-organised servants' wing or 'offices' was essential to ensure the efficient running of a Victorian country house. At Brodsworth, the Servants' Wing with its numerous rooms extends at a right angle to the main block of the house at the back, with the Kitchen placed at the junction of the two blocks. This meant there was only a short distance for food to be carried to the Dining Room, so that it could arrive reasonably hot. However, it also meant that servants had to carry food and dirty dishes across one of the main family corridors and vistas through the house, an unusual breach of the principle of keeping the servants out of sight.

The Kitchen was served by the adjacent Scullery, Still Room and Larder, and there were keeping cellars for meat, dairy produce, beer and wine. The two head servants had their own rooms, the Butler's Pantry and Housekeeper's Room. The butler and footmen slept downstairs and the female servants upstairs, with the Housekeeper's bedroom at the head of the servants' staircase. The Servants' Hall was where all the servants met to have their meals. A courtyard at the back served these busy 'offices', and there were separate buildings for the Laundry, Game Larder and Stables.

When the house was first built it was heated by coal fires and was lit by gas, supplied by its own gasworks in the grounds. Although there were eight water closets for the family and servants, there were originally only two bathrooms: the housemaids would have had to

carry water for washing in cans to all the rooms. Sinks for the waste water were conveniently placed near each end of the main bedroom corridor. A system of bells wired to boards in the servants' corridors summoned the servants.

Over the years these arrangements were altered. Electricity was introduced by Charles and Constance Thellusson in about 1913, when many of the light fittings were replaced. The Grant-Daltons later installed central heating in the corridors, an Aga cooker, and washbasins in many of the bedrooms. All this meant that fewer servants were needed, so that many of the rooms in the Servants' Wing gradually fell out of use.

One of the memorable vistas through the house, from the Entrance and Inner Halls through the South Hall to the West Hall. This is one of a series of photographs taken in 1910 to mark the Silver Wedding of Charles and Constance Thellusson

LEFT *One of the washbasins detailed in the specification for the building of the house in 1861*

BELOW *Some of the cans used for carrying hot water*

The Dolphin off Amsterdam, painted by Ludolf Backhuysen in about 1668. This magnificent seapiece was Charles Thellusson's most costly purchase, at 650 guineas. The sideboard is one of the early nineteenth-century pieces of furniture in the house, while the massive silver tankards date from 1873

YORKSHIRE ARCHAEOLOGICAL SOCIETY

The beginning of Lapworths' twenty-three page bill for furnishing the house

Decoration and furnishings

As with its architecture, the original interior decoration of Brodsworth reflected Charles Sabine Thellusson's taste, his predilection for the Italian, and perhaps the influence of the mysterious Casentini. It also reveals the typical Victorian desire for comfort and opulence, which was well answered by the new but conventional furnishings provided by Lapworths. The interior we see today, however, is not simply that of a house of the 1860s. The Thellussons brought to Brodsworth many of the contents of their Brighton home, and fittings from the old Brodsworth Hall were also incorporated. Over the years there have also been many redecorations, and both additions to and losses from the contents. Like most country houses, Brodsworth contains a mixture of old and new.

The detailed building specification of 1861 clearly shows how the fireplaces, windows, and even the depth of the skirtings and cornices were carefully graded for different parts of the house. The skirtings, for example, range from 46cm (18 inches) in the Drawing Rooms to 20cm (8 inches) in the Servants' Corridor. The specification also gives general instructions for the interior decoration, such as that the halls

and circulation spaces were to be 'painted 5 times and finished in imitation marble by hand'. The very fine painted ceiling in the Drawing Rooms and rich wallpapers of the Morning Room are not mentioned in the surviving records, but are assumed to be early additions. Wallpapers were specified for all the upstairs rooms, and cheaper ones for the servants' bedrooms.

All the carpets, upholstery and a large amount of furniture were provided by the firm of Lapworth Brothers of Old Bond Street, London, whose total bill at the end of 1863 amounted to £7,282, just under a quarter of the total sum spent on the building works. The bill shows how the main reception rooms received the finest and most expensive furnishings, the bedrooms less costly ones, and the servants the cheapest, although they were still comfortably provided for. There were a fascinating number of gradations in the carpets provided, from the most expensive hand-knotted 'Extra Superfine Real Axminster' in the Drawing Rooms, through 'Superfine Real Axminsters' in the Dining Room and Library, to mere 'Real Axminsters' in the halls and corridors. Machine-made Brussels carpets were produced for the Morning Room, School Room and first-floor bedrooms.

Lapworths created sumptuous silk and velvet curtains for the main reception rooms, and a set of sixteen heavy red wool curtains for the halls. They also provided a variety of chintz curtains and bed hangings upstairs, and chintz covers throughout the house.

The furniture supplied by Lapworths included important pieces such as the Dining Room table and chairs, the Billiard Room seating, and the mahogany bedroom furniture. These give an overall visual unity to the house. However, there are many earlier pieces, including a group of rosewood furniture by T & G Seddon of London. There are also many

A detail of the 'Extra Superfine Real Axminster' made by Lapworths for the Drawing Rooms

later additions, such as the carpets and curtains in the Dining Room, Library, and most of the bedrooms.

One of the dominating decorative elements of the halls and corridors is Charles Thellusson's large collection of Italian marble sculpture, consisting of fifteen large figures and eight smaller ones. He bought all the figures at the Dublin International Exhibition of 1865, where all but two of them were being exhibited through Casentini, acting as an agent for other sculptors. Casentini also supplied ornaments for the garden comprising fifteen classical figures, eight greyhounds, several urns and the fountain.

The collection reveals Thellusson's taste for contemporary sculpture, with its often sentimental subject matter and concentration on intricate details and textures. He chose a mixture of light-hearted subjects such as a girl with her spaniel, and more serious ones such as *Education* and the Virgin and Child. Almost all the sculptures are of female figures, often with revealing drapery – 'poor cold ladies', as Sylvia Grant-Dalton called them. Indeed the general distaste in later years for nineteenth-century sculpture means that the collection at Brodsworth is rare in having survived in the setting for which it was purchased in the 1860s.

In addition, Charles Thellusson bought a small number of paintings for his new house. He had inherited two magnificent family portraits, one of his grandmother and father by Sir Thomas Lawrence, and the other of Madame Thellusson by Nicolas de Largillière. Charles's marriage to Georgiana Theobald in 1850 had also brought a significant group of portraits and equestrian paintings into the family.

To this collection Charles Thellusson added several seventeenth-century Dutch paintings. He obviously valued them highly, hanging them in the Dining Room with the best portraits and mentioning them specifically in his will as 'heirlooms'.

Charles also acquired a few paintings of 'genre' or everyday scenes, popular in the Victorian period. There are in addition several paintings of dogs, many of them by members of the family, and a few paintings which have come to the house in more recent years. Brodsworth thus has a typical country house picture collection, ranging widely in date, subject and quality, but reflecting the family's interests.

The interest and value of Brodsworth's interior lies not only in the specific areas of paintings, sculpture and furniture, and in the fact that so much survives from the 1860s, but also in the accumulation of so many often ordinary objects which reflect the lives and history of a family over several generations.

ABOVE The Swinging Girl *by Pietro Magni, 1865. This was purchased directly from the Dublin Exhibition Company, rather than through Casentini, and is visible in a photograph taken at the exhibition* (ABOVE LEFT*)*

The Entrance and Inner Halls

The Entrance Hall is the first of Brodsworth's memorable sequence of halls and corridors. It leads directly into the Inner Hall, and from there to the South Hall and on to the West and North Halls. Together they provided a generous and impressive space in which to welcome guests and to circulate between the main rooms, and could even be used as rooms themselves.

In keeping with the exterior of the house, the halls provide a strong Italianate setting. They are united visually by the painted marbling of the walls, the scagliola (imitation marble) columns and pilasters, the floors of Brodsworth stone decorated with Minton tiles, and the crimson carpets and curtains whose borders complement the tiles.

The walls are intended to suggest many different coloured marbles arranged in panels. The original varnish has darkened with age, the paint has suffered from continuous flaking, and over the years the surface has been regularly cleaned and repaired. During English Heritage's conservation programme, it was decided that until the sequence of the decoration was better understood, both the damage and subsequent overpainting should remain.

The furnishings have also suffered from age and use. The Axminster carpets in the first two halls are therefore accurate reproductions, but the original carpets supplied by Lapworths in 1863 can be seen on the stairs and in the further halls.

RIGHT The harmonising borders of Lapworths' carpets and curtains and the surrounding Mintons' encaustic tiles which can be seen throughout the halls

OPPOSITE The Inner and Entrance Halls, with their combination of marbling, sculptures and reproduction crimson carpets

BELOW Deceptive decoration: a scagliola pilaster and paintwork imitating yellow Siena and other marbles in the Entrance Hall

Standing out against the colourful decoration are the white marble figures of Charles Thellusson's collection of mid-nineteenth-century Italian sculpture, bought in 1865. Two of the most impressive figures are in the Staircase Hall: *Education*, or a girl teaching a young boy to read, by Giuseppe Lazzerini, and Pietro Magni's *The Swinging Girl*. Between the columns linking the two halls are figures of a young girl and boy representing Spring and Autumn, as well as two signalling cannons from yachts, reflecting one of the family's abiding interests. The two paintings of racehorses situated above the doors reveal another family pastime and give a foretaste of the equestrian paintings which are such a feature of Brodsworth.

The Morning Room

From the Entrance Hall a door to the left leads past a water closet to the Morning Room. This intimate, richly decorated room, furnished with comfortable chairs and writing tables, was a place in which the family could spend quiet time.

The wallpaper, which is original, is printed and gilded to resemble stamped leather. The crimson velvet curtains have also survived, and will be reinstated after undergoing extensive conservation. The room initially had a 'Turkey design' Brussels carpet, but this was replaced as early as the 1890s; the present carpet dates from

The Morning Room

1904. Original furniture to have survived includes the leather-topped desk, Regency inlaid table and caned chairs.

The portrait over the fireplace is of the builder of Brodsworth Hall, Charles Sabine Thellusson, in his cavalry uniform. The room also contains many paintings of dogs, some of them pets of the Thellussons such as the small terrier, Prairie Prince, and 'Coup', the white terrier shown on a fur-covered chair, who is buried in the pets' graveyard in the garden. Some of these dog paintings are by members of the family. The architectural watercolour on the easel is of the house, and was probably painted in the early 1860s.

Georgiana Theobald, painted by Margaret Carpenter in 1850, the year of her marriage to Charles Sabine Thellusson. The pair to this portrait, on the left of the sideboard, is of Georgiana's sister in 1840

The Dining Room

The Dining Room at Brodsworth, as in all country houses, was intended as much for show as for eating. Charles Sabine placed his most important paintings in this room, as well as family silver and new furniture. The arrangement of the furniture and paintings remains much as it was in the 1860s.

The door near the Regency sideboard gives access, across the main corridor, to the serving hatch at the back of the Kitchen. The fine eighteenth-century fireplace was reused from the old house, but was given a nineteenth-century brass and steel insert. The decoration of the room is surprisingly plain. The ceiling is heavily moulded, but the walls are simply painted. Nevertheless, the room would originally have had a much richer appearance, with a crimson 'Indian' design Axminster carpet and crimson velvet curtains. The massive dining table and set of eighteen leather upholstered chairs were supplied by Lapworths.

A major change in the appearance of the room was made in 1907 when Charles and Constance Thellusson replaced the original carpet with the present 'Turkey' carpet, bought from Maples for £102. A few years later, when they introduced electricity to the house, the original gas chandelier was replaced by the present electric one.

The Dining Room contains some of the finest paintings in the house. Charles Sabine hung portraits of his own and his wife's family here. The large portrait by Sir Thomas

LEFT *The Dining Room, with the furniture supplied by Lapworths, family portraits and Dutch paintings. The large portrait is by Sir Thomas Lawrence of Charles Sabine's grandmother and father as a boy*

Lawrence is of his grandmother, Sabine Thellusson, with his father, Charles, as a young boy dressed in red. Above the fireplace is a portrait by Philip Reinagle of his wife's grandfather, John Theobald.

Charles Thellusson added to these his major purchases of seventeenth-century Dutch paintings. These include the large seapiece by Backhuysen which hangs above the sideboard, and a smaller painting by the same artist to the right of the fireplace depicting the landing of William of Orange at Scheveningham on the Dutch coast. To the left of the Lawrence is a landscape with a hawking party by Wynants and Wouvermans, and on the other side by the window is a moonlit canal scene by Van der Neer. (Both the larger Backhuysen and the Wynants and Wouvermans have kindly been loaned to Brodsworth by Mr Ronald Williams.)

The South Hall

The walls of the South Hall were originally hung with the same crimson silk as the Drawing Rooms. This would have contrasted much more vividly with the yellow or Siena scagliola columns than the present yellow silk damask which replaced it in about 1914. The room contains a number of eighteenth-century gilt armchairs and sofas which are part of the large set in the Drawing Rooms.

The pair of large sculptures by Giuseppe Lazzerini are of a *Nymph going to Bathe*, dipping her toe into a stream, and *Vanity*, who has unfortunately lost the mirror she once held. The fireplace and doors to either side date from the eighteenth century and were brought from the previous Brodsworth Hall.

ABOVE *The South Hall once contained an 'American organ' and this 1902 Monarch gramophone (photographed about 1910)*

BELOW *Sculptures set amongst columns and the crimson carpets and curtains of the South Hall. The walls were originally also covered in crimson silk*

The Billiard Room

By the mid-nineteenth century a Billiard Room was considered essential for gentlemen's entertainment in a country house. The one at Brodsworth retains much of its original character.

The massive table with its slate bed and accessories was supplied by Cox and Yemen of London. A leather-bound book records the game scores since the 1880s. The leather upholstered seating, with its combination of sofas and armchairs, was specially designed by Lapworths, who also provided linoleum for the floor and carpeting for the raised platforms. In 1880 a local firm, Anelays, replaced these with the present Wilton carpet and 'Silentium' linoleum, with its design of parquet floor and ivy leaf border. The room always had a ventilation problem, no doubt worsened by cigar smoke, and Anelays also installed the two large ventilation hatches.

The furnishings are complemented by a remarkable collection of early nineteenth-century equestrian paintings. Five of them are by James Ward, three by James Barenger, and the one over the scoreboard by the elder Herring. They were collected by the Theobald family, and came to Brodsworth through the marriage in 1850 of Georgiana Theobald to Charles Sabine Thellusson. Her grandfather John Theobald had bred many successful racehorses at his stud at Stockwell in Essex; the large painting by Barenger over the fireplace depicts *The Theobald Stud*.

Theobald clearly admired Ward's work, purchasing several paintings by him at an auction in 1821. These included the pair of paintings of stallions on either side of the fireplace, and the impressive and romantic *Walton* opposite the door, where a stallion is shown having bolted from his rider. Theobald

ABOVE LEFT Walton, *an unusually dramatic portrayal of a racehorse by James Ward in 1821*

OPPOSITE *The Billiard Room in 1995, with its original furnishings.* The Theobald Stud, *painted by James Barenger in 1825, hangs above the fireplace*

ABOVE *The leather-bound volume in which scores have been recorded since the 1880s*

BELOW *The scoreboard*

RIGHT *The Doncaster Cup, won by Rataplan in 1855. The silver trophy, depicting an episode from Walter Scott's* Ivanhoe, *can be seen in the Family Exhibition upstairs*

later commissioned paintings personally from Ward, including the portrait of himself with his successful racehorse Rockingham which hangs to the right of the scoreboard.

On the left of the board is a painting by Harry Hall of the famous racehorse Rataplan. It was bred in the Theobald stud and acquired by Charles Thellusson after the marriage of his son to Georgiana Theobald. Rataplan's winnings are said to have solved some of his financial difficulties, and the Doncaster Cup he won in 1855 is on display upstairs.

The only portrait in the room (over the door) is of Peter Thellusson, the eldest son of Charles Sabine, on his yacht.

The Drawing Rooms

These are the most splendid rooms at Brodsworth, intended for grand entertaining. Silks, gilding, mirrors, marble and a colourful ceiling and carpet combine to create a vibrant yet delicate interior. A more intimate area is formed at one end by the white scagliola columns: for many years a grand piano stood here, making it a little music room. In the 1930s the Drawing Rooms provided an impressive setting for the local Hunt Ball.

A great deal of the original scheme survives, including the two 'handsome glass chandeliers in the Venetian style for gas' from Lapworths and the marble fireplaces. The decorative ceiling is complemented by the original hand-knotted carpet, described by Lapworths as an 'Extra Superfine Real Axminster Carpet to Special Design, Italian Scrolls ornament and flowers'. At £367.10s this was the most expensive carpet in the house. The strong colours have faded but the section of carpet in the smaller Drawing Room, which was for some years used in another room, gives a suggestion of their original brightness.

Lapworths also supplied, in the late eighteenth-century French style which was then

ABOVE *The crimson silk damask wall coverings in the Drawing Rooms. Originally the same silk was used in the South Hall*

RIGHT *The Drawing Rooms. A view of the rooms in the 1880s can be seen on page 10*

The border of the Drawing Room ceiling, delicately painted in an Italianate style

fashionable, the gilt woodwork of the splendid mirrors, the console table and the window cornices, with their 'lambrequins of super crimson Lyons lampas' or shaped silk pelmets.

The set of late eighteenth-century gilt chairs and sofas was brought from the old house and reupholstered by Lapworths in silk 'lampas'. They also re-covered the massive and typically Victorian central 'ottoman sociable' in another design of crimson silk. Photographs show loose coverings on the furniture and muslin sun curtains and blinds to protect the expensive and delicate silks and carpet. However, these were not always used so the textiles are particularly fragile and have required extensive conservation.

Lapworths supplied the large circular inlaid satinwood table and the table veneered with tortoiseshell and brass or 'Boulle' work. The pair of small rosewood card tables are part of an interesting group of furniture in the house made by T & G Seddon of London in the early years of the nineteenth century.

The Drawing Rooms were once densely filled with ornaments (many under glass domes), plants and flowers, and had three marble statues in front of the window pier glasses. Some of the ornaments remain, such as the French porcelain vases and clock, and the little marble figures of children.

The West Hall

The corridor outside the Drawing Rooms combines the richest painted decoration with a dense grouping of sculptures backed by gilt-framed mirrors, making it the climax of the painted halls. It has an arcade with white painted pilasters, decorative plasterwork and stencilled patterns.

The sculptures include three versions of famous works: the classical *Venus de' Medici*

with a dolphin at her feet; *Eve with Cain and Abel* by Debay; and *The Virgin Mary* after Raphael. Near the window are two figures by Pietro Franchi, of a girl playing with her dog and another reading. Finally, the long vista from the Inner Hall is terminated by the marble figure of a *Sleeping Girl* by Giosue Argenti. This is dimly lit from behind by the large internal window, which has a delicately painted glass border with cherubs depicting the seasons.

Around the corner is the North Hall, containing three further sculptures: a copy of the *Venus Italica* by Canova and figures of a peasant girl and a shepherdess. On one side hang three paintings by William Perry dating from the 1860s depicting children in rural scenes, perhaps the most typically Victorian paintings in the house.

The West Hall

The painted decoration in the West Hall. Even the stencilled designs are marbled

ABOVE RIGHT *A corner of the Library in 1990*

ABOVE *Part of the richly painted glass border of the window which sheds light from the Library into the West Hall*

The Library

The Library has always been a well-used room, particularly by Sylvia Grant-Dalton in her later years. It contains over 1000 leather-bound volumes of history, the classics and literature, most of which were inherited or acquired by Charles Sabine Thellusson. His eldest son Peter also added regularly to the library in the 1880s and '90s, pursuing wide-ranging literary interests including travel and photography.

The original Axminster carpet, 'of Persian design' with a green background, can just be seen at the edges of the room; as it became worn out first one and then another carpet was laid on top. The original curtains of rich green 'Utrecht velvet' with gold and green trimmings sadly have not survived; together with the carpet and wallpaper they would have created a sumptuous interior.

The portrait above the fireplace is of Madame Sarah Thellusson. She was the mother of Peter Thellusson, who made the famous will which eventually enabled his great-grandson to build Brodsworth Hall (see page 2). The portrait is by the French artist Nicolas de Largillière and is dated 1725, shortly after Sarah's marriage to the banker Isaac Thellusson.

The two portraits of gentlemen in the manner of Rembrandt were probably collected by Charles Sabine Thellusson. The other large portrait is of Mrs Sarah Theobald, Charles Sabine Thellusson's mother-in-law. It was painted in 1832 by James Ward, the artist of many of the equestrian paintings in the Billiard Room.

The furniture has been changed around many times over the years. At one time it included a rosewood upright piano, which was sold in 1946. The circular rosewood table with ormolou or gilt brass mounts is by Seddon, and the rosewood cabinet near the door also dates from the early nineteenth century.

Water closet

Next door to the Library is one of the 'Principal Water Closets' with mahogany seat and marble-topped washstand which were provided when the house was built.

The Lathe Room

The final room leading off from the main halls was originally called 'Captain Thellusson's Lathe Room': here Charles Sabine Thellusson pursued his hobby of wood-turning. On his death the contents of the room included his lathe, circular saw, work bench and tools, the central table with drawers, and several ships' models which he may have made. When the Grant-Daltons came to the hall in 1932 Sylvia Grant-Dalton is said to have taken a dislike to the stuffed birds

and animals throughout the house, and gathered them all into this room. Unfortunately they have since suffered from both moth and damp, and many are in a very poor condition.

Stairs and first-floor corridor

The West Stairs take you to the first floor. The painted marbling is continued in the wide corridor linking all the bedrooms. It is at its simplest at the top of the stairs, but as the corridor reaches the more important family bedrooms, pilasters and a decorative dado (lower portion of the walls) are introduced. The decoration is at its most elaborate on the landing outside the principal bedrooms, which is a continuation of the main stairs.

The marbling is complemented by the crimson and gold star-patterned carpet. Although the design is almost exactly the same as in the hand-knotted Axminsters downstairs, cheaper machine-woven Brussels or loop-pile carpet was used. The present carpet is a reproduction of the original, which had worn through to the floorboards in places.

The enormous linen cupboard was supplied by Lapworths; handwritten labels on the shelves record its former contents. The corridor was originally densely furnished with tables, chairs and cabinets, including the large mahogany wardrobe and the glass-fronted cabinet, both made by Seddon in the early nineteenth century. The paintings include small works by Ward, Barenger and Herring, as well as works by members of the Thellusson family; Aline, the elder daughter of Charles Sabine, painted the pair of landscapes with cattle and sheep, and the group of two dogs.

Bedrooms

There are sixteen rooms on the first floor (not all on view), which have always been identified by a simple numbering system. Suites of rooms were unified originally by having the same carpets, curtains and upholstery, but the original schemes have been lost through frequent refurbishments. The washbasins that can be seen in many of the bedrooms were installed by the Grant-Daltons in about 1960.

Lapworths provided a large amount of mahogany furniture for the bedrooms, including four half-tester (canopied) beds, marble-topped washstands, chests of drawers and armchairs. There are also some earlier pieces of furniture,

The hand-blocked wallpaper in the Library imitates stamped leather; the same design is used in the Morning Room, but with some of the colours reversed

LEFT *A pair of albino peacocks in the Lathe Room*

such as early nineteenth-century washstands and writing tables.

The first rooms you see, at the west end of the first floor, are the less important bedrooms originally used by the younger members of the family or by visitors. They contain eighteenth-century marble fireplaces from the old house, while the 'Best Bedrooms' were given new ones. It is intended that two of these rooms will be refurnished once the conservation of their contents has been completed.

The rooms were served by a **Bathroom**, which can be seen by turning right from the stairs and then right again through a door. Like the bedrooms it has lost its original decoration, but contains an interesting 'commode'. Opposite it on the main corridor is a pair of bedrooms, and then a suite with a small central dressing room. The corner room now contains an exhibition about members of the family and

their interests. The first furnished room is Bedroom 8, about half way down the corridor.

Bedroom 8

This was called the 'Large Spare Room' by Lapworths, and was intended to be the most impressive visitors' room. It was completely refurbished by Charles and Constance Thellusson in 1904, but was little used after Charles's death in 1919, and gradually fell into disrepair. It is shown in this abandoned condition, having undergone minimal conservation.

The magnificent boat-shaped bed, or 'lit en bateau', probably dates from the 1850s, although it is in the style of early nineteenth-century French beds. The Thellussons must have already owned it, since in 1863 Lapworths only supplied new hangings. In 1904 Hall &

Bedroom 8 with its boat-shaped bed, photographed before conservation in 1990. The room has been abandoned since 1919

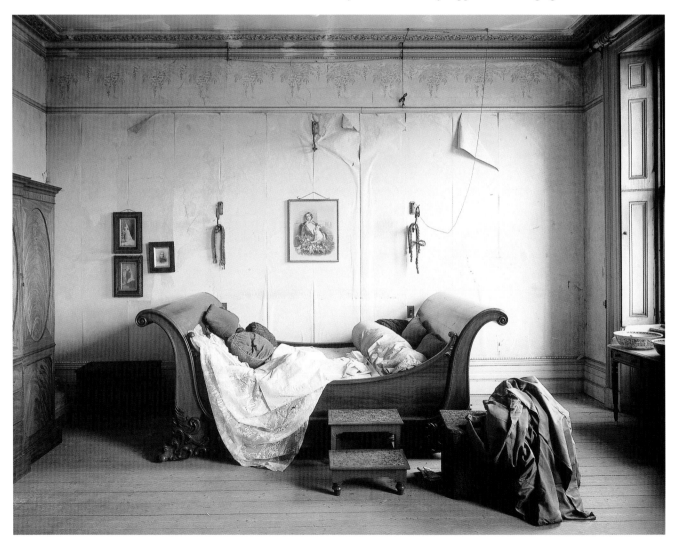

Armitage of Wakefield provided new chintz hangings and window curtains with a purple design, and a new carpet. They also whitened the woodwork and repapered the rooms, darkening the flowers in the frieze to match the chintz. The sagging wallpaper was later secured with steel tacks, which have been left in position.

Amongst the other furnishings in the room are a fine eighteenth-century mahogany press or cupboard, and two of Lapworths' washstands. There is also an interesting 'Double Action Mechanical Bed' dating from 1885, with its original gold upholstery.

Bedrooms 7-4

The four interconnecting rooms at the east end of the corridor were described by Lapworths as 'Mrs Thellusson's suite of four rooms'. The two central bedrooms for the master and mistress of the house are flanked by smaller dressing rooms on each side. Lapworths originally furnished them all with a green patterned Brussels carpet, matching Axminster hearth rugs, and French chintz curtains and upholstery. However, each room now has a completely different furnishing scheme.

Bedroom 7 (Dressing Room)

This room was used as a dressing room, and subsequently as a bedroom by the young Pamela Grant-Dalton. It has lost much of its furniture, but the prints, paintings and model yacht reflect the family's maritime interests.

Bedroom 6

This room seems always to have been used by the lady of the house, and was Sylvia Grant-Dalton's bedroom until her death in 1988. Her scheme comprised pink wallpaper and a variety

Some of the few remaining Victorian toys in Bedroom 5

of earlier chintzes brought from other rooms for use on the late nineteenth-century bed and at the windows. The armchair is upholstered in the crimson wool damask originally used in the Nurseries.

Bedroom 5

Traditionally this was the bedroom of the head of the household. It was originally supplied with a bed with white chintz and muslin draperies, but by 1931 this had been replaced by a large brass bed which remained in the room until after Charles Grant-Dalton's death. Most of the furniture came from Lapworths, but the carpet was provided by Hall & Armitage for Bedroom 8, and was cut down to fit this room by the Grant-Daltons.

Bedroom 4 (Dressing Room)

This room, used for most of its history as a dressing room, retains much of its original furniture, including a dressing table, washstand, low clothes press and fine central table. The Axminster carpet supplied by Hall & Armitage for Charles Thellusson's 'own Dressing Room' in 1904 can be seen at the edges of the room. In addition to the barometers, the room used to contain several marine chronometers and a telescope. Many of the photographs date from Charles and Constance Thellusson's time. The bathroom next door was updated by the Grant-Daltons.

LEFT *A model yacht found propped on a towel rail in Bedroom 7*

BELOW *One of Lapworths' sturdy pieces of bedroom furniture*

'Haydocks' Horse', with stirrups and interior springs, for taking indoor exercise. It stands amongst other objects that were relegated to the Servants' Wing when no longer required

A late nineteenth-century zinc-lined refrigerator. Ice could be packed into compartments in the top, and the melted water drained from the tap at the bottom. It was superseded by an electric deep-freeze in the Larder

Before returning across the main landing, look into the **Sitting Room** opposite. This large room directly over the Entrance Hall was the Day Nursery for Charles Sabine Thellusson's children. In his son Charles's time it became 'Mrs Thellusson's Sitting Room'. The Grant-Daltons also used it as a sitting room, making it more comfortable by bringing in the silk curtains and part of the carpet from the Drawing Rooms. It is now used as a sitting room for visitors and as an Education Room.

The main landing provides a good view of the grand staircase and hall below, lit by a huge lantern. This has its original etched glass on the two long sides but the two shorter sides were replaced with perspex after being shattered by the report of a Bofors gun stationed on the roof during the Second World War.

A door on the right at the head of the corridor leads past one of the original water closets and through the baize-covered doors which separate the main family rooms from the Nursery area behind the main stairs. The first room on the right was originally the **Governess's Bedroom**. It now contains an exhibition about the servants and the running of a house such as Brodsworth. You then return to continue down the stairs and through a further baize-covered door into the Servants' Wing.

Servants' Wing: first floor

The Servants' Wing abuts the main block of the house at right angles. The first floor originally housed the female servants, with the male servants sleeping downstairs. From the 1860s until about 1918 there were approximately ten female servants, including the housekeeper, cook, housemaids, kitchen and scullery maids. In the twentieth century the number of servants declined to just one in Sylvia Grant-Dalton's later years. The servants' rooms were used increasingly for storage and gradually fell into disuse.

The Servants' Wing was built on a smaller scale than the main house. Many fittings were reused from the eighteenth-century house, including the small-paned sash windows, the doors and fireplaces. The servants' bedrooms were originally quite comfortably furnished with carpets and furniture from Lapworths. With the exception of the Housekeeper's Bedroom, most of the rooms contained two iron bedsteads and a pine wardrobe, washstand and sometimes two chests of drawers, grained to imitate better woods. Although much of the furniture survives, all the original carpets, curtains, bedding and most small objects have been lost. While three of the bedrooms are shown as lumber rooms, much as they were found, the lumber has not been replaced in the other three to reveal the original furniture surviving underneath.

At the far right of the Landing is the **Housekeeper's Bedroom**. This originally had slightly better-quality furnishings than the other rooms, including a Brussels carpet, damask curtains, and a mahogany table and washstand supplied by Lapworths. By 1952 the room was occupied by the butler, but soon afterwards a flat was made for him downstairs and the room was used for storage.

At the head of the corridor leading to the other rooms the remains of the bell system can be seen. On the right is the **Housemaids' Sitting Room**, which was once furnished with several chairs, a table and cupboards containing crockery. By the 1950s it had become the Laundry Room. The present contents of the room, including the sink, clothes' dolly and washing machine, reflect this change in use. The grained cupboard to the left of the fireplace opens to reveal a fold-out bed for servants – a rare survival. The elegant early nineteenth-century painted Gothic chairs, possibly from a bedroom or even a garden building, must have been relegated to the Servants' Wing when they were no longer fashionable.

The room next to this, decorated with blue distemper, has always been used for storage or lumber. The remaining three rooms on show were originally bedrooms containing two beds each. One was later used to store all the ceramic toilet services, after basins had been plumbed into the bedrooms. The two beyond were used by the Grant-Daltons' staff. In the cross passage is a huge linen cupboard supplied by Lapworths, containing bedlinen. There are still faded handwritten labels on the shelves recording its contents. The four rooms at the head of the corridor, once bedrooms, are now used as offices and storage space.

Servants' Wing: ground floor

At the bottom of the stairs go straight ahead, to the **Larder**. It has many shelves, a cold slab and a cupboard with perforated zinc doors for storing food. There is a large pestle and mortar and a later deep freeze. The window at the back sheds light into what was once the housemaids' cupboard but is now the lift shaft.

PHOTOGRAPHS COURTESY OF THE EDWARDS FAMILY

Some of the servants in Charles and Constance Thellusson's day. TOP LEFT *The wedding of the cook, Martha Locke, and chauffeur, George Raper, in about 1915.* TOP RIGHT *Alfred Edwards (Alf) in about 1915. As well as serving as valet and later chauffeur to Charles Thellusson, Alf was an amateur photographer and took most of the photographs of servants shown here.* CENTRE RIGHT *Caroline Palmer, who came to Brodsworth as a scullery maid in 1907, and worked her way up to become cook in 1915. She married Alfred Edwards the following year.* CENTRE *Miss Jane Langton, the formidable housekeeper who held sway at Brodsworth from 1895 to 1935.* CENTRE LEFT *Gamekeepers and groundsmen in front of the kennels in about 1915.* BOTTOM *The indoor servants, photographed in the snow in about 1914*

The Kitchen

This is reached on the right after passing the foot of the stairs again. The cavernous top-lit room with its ranges and dressers illustrates the space and equipment required to cater for a well-to-do Victorian family and its staff. From the 1860s until at least 1919 it was the domain of the resident cook and kitchen maid, assisted by scullery maids who washed all the dishes and helped prepare vegetables in the Scullery opposite.

The Kitchen must have seemed antiquated and inconvenient to the Grant-Daltons on their arrival in 1932 and they abandoned it in favour of the smaller Still Room. When the house was requisitioned by the Army during the Second World War the Kitchen briefly came back into use to cater for the officers billeted here. Traces of this last occupation can be seen in the black-out blinds beneath the skylight and a notice with air-raid precautions stuck to the back of the door. After the war the room was used for storage, while the ranges and utensils gathered dust and rust. The Kitchen is shown in its abandoned state (its contents having been gently cleaned), illustrating the fate of many huge Victorian kitchens in the twentieth century.

Many of the original fittings and contents can still be seen. Both the substantial main 'Eagle' range and its smaller companion to the left were made and installed by Farr and Sons of Doncaster. Farrs regularly attended the house to maintain the ranges and carry out repairs such as retinning pans. The ranges are flanked by a steam closet or boiler to the right and a long hot plate. The sliding serving hatch in the far corner enabled food to be taken to the Dining Room by the shortest possible route. The grained dressers were brought from the old house, and the central table was supplied by Lapworths.

The Butler's Pantry

Turning right outside the Kitchen, you come to the Butler's Pantry at the end of the corridor. A door at the far side of the room gave the butler easy access to the front door and the main part of the house. The room was used by the butler for storing and cleaning silver plate, cutlery and glasses. Almost the whole of one wall is taken by a massive cupboard with sliding doors, originally installed for £10.

The remaining servants' rooms on the ground floor now contain a shop and tea rooms. The shop is in the **Servants' Hall** where all the servants once took their meals. By the 1950s it had lost its original furniture and become a lumber or store room. Across the corridor, one of the tea rooms was the **Housekeeper's Room**. One wall is entirely taken by a huge cupboard for china and table linen. The room was originally comfortably furnished with a mahogany table and chairs, and continued to be used as a sitting room for staff until very recently.

Kent's Patent Knife Cleaner of 1903

Part of the large collection of pewter and copper moulds for jellies, patties and ices, and other utensils

The present kitchen, serving room and the other two tea rooms were once the butler's and footman's bedrooms, Gun Room and a household store. By about 1970 they had been converted into a flat for the butler. The **Aga Kitchen** was originally the Still Room, used for making preserves and confectionery. A door near the Aga leads to the original **Scullery**, still used today for cleaning equipment and storage. All these rooms are linked by a wide corridor decorated on the lower part of the walls to imitate granite or mottled stone.

You can leave the house either by the door at the end of this corridor, or by the door beside the shop, which leads into the service yard. From the yard, a short path through the trees leads to the gardens.

The Kitchen, though abandoned since 1919, still contains a wide range of copper and iron pans and other cooking equipment. Against the back wall is a 'meat screen' – a cupboard on castors – which could be wheeled in front of the range to keep food and plates hot

LEFT *The capacious 'Eagle Range', made by Farr and Sons of Doncaster, with two ovens to each side of the central fire*

THE GARDENS

STEPHEN ANDERTON AND PETER GORDON-SMITH

When old Brodsworth Hall was pulled down and the present house built in the 1860s, a new garden was developed around the house. Despite some replanting around the turn of the nineteenth century and a gradual decline in maintenance thereafter, the remains are still evidently a product of the third quarter of the nineteenth century.

The gardens cover 6 hectares (15 acres) and are set within what was once extensive parkland (not in the care of English Heritage). Typical of their period, they comprise contrasted areas of high formality, of seasonal bedding and dense clipped shrubberies with areas of studied, rustic prettiness, of climbing roses, arbours and varied vistas, together with a fountain, a cascade, marble statuary and various quaint garden buildings.

As the number of garden staff declined in the latter half of the twentieth century, sections of the garden were abandoned to nature, and woodland areas were allowed to encroach and choke the border shrubberies. However, the essential structure of the nineteenth-century garden remained unaltered, and the gardens are now being progressively restored to their appearance in their heyday.

The setting of the hall

Like many nineteenth-century houses, Brodsworth Hall sits at the centre of its own secluding woodlands and shrubberies. Woods of beech, oak, lime, sycamore and yew hide the house from all unwanted views. A few of the trees, notably some splendid cedars, date from the time of the earlier hall, which stood a little to the north of the present building between the stables and Brodsworth church.

The main drive passes through the woods, with their clipped evergreen border shrubberies, and swings past the lawns to reveal the east front of the house. To the south the principal façade of the house enjoys an open aspect, overlooking lawns and hedges into the park. Beyond the house to the west lie the principal features of the pleasure grounds – the flower garden and the Grove.

To the south and west the house sits on a raised terrace of grass banks, punctuated at regular intervals by steps adorned with shallow urns (tazzas) and greyhounds, all of marble. The theme of sculpture, so prominent inside the house, is carried through into the garden: marble statues of female figures in the classical tradition set in niches in the yew hedges punctuate the boundary of the lawns. The garden statuary was supplied new from Italy in 1866 by Chevalier Casentini, who had a hand in the design of the setting. The entire presentation of the hall is simple and formal, with no planting to clutter its appearance other than the colourful plants in the tazzas, without which no Victorian garden was complete. This simplicity belies the varied features to be seen in the pleasure grounds.

OPPOSITE A view across the flower garden, shrubberies and croquet lawns towards the hall

LEFT This nineteenth-century photograph shows the formal gardens shortly after they were laid out in the 1860s. Note that the sculptural urns had not yet been added to the roof of the hall

One of the Italian white marble statues, representing one of the Muses, supplied by Chevalier Casentini in 1866

The summerhouse, built in the 1860s, commands views of the formal gardens, the Grove and the hall. The undergrowth around it has been cleared as part of the garden conservation

The pets' cemetery, where the family dogs – and a parrot or two – lie buried. The stones date from 1894 to 1988

The vibrantly coloured flower garden

The flower garden

To the west of the house are lawns for croquet (a game developed in the 1860s) and, masking the flower garden, a pair of substantial shrubberies that have been replanted around the two cedar trees. The flower garden, laid out around the fountain supplied by Casentini, is of formal design, consisting of symmetrical beds cut into the turf. The formality is enhanced by a striking pair of monkey puzzle trees on either side of the fountain. Such flower gardens were a favourite device of the period, and provided an opportunity for the head gardeners of the day to experiment with brightly coloured bedding schemes and contemporary theories on colour coordination. It was commonplace to provide two bedding schemes per year – one for spring and one for summer – but wealthy owners could afford to ring the changes even more frequently. The colour in the flower garden at Brodsworth forms a strong contrast with the rest of the garden, which concentrates heavily on the clipped shrubberies of mixed evergreens – such as laurel, box, holly and yew – popular in the Victorian age.

The Grove

From the southern end of the flower garden the summerhouse, a temple-like structure raised up on a contrived mound, is visible. A discreet path leads around the side of the mound into secluded woodland, where the pets' cemetery lies. Here the headstones of family pets date from 1894 to 1988. The summerhouse marks the beginning of the Grove, an enchanting part of the garden. This is essentially a quarry garden, set amongst tall sheltering trees, covering several acres and containing a number of interesting features. It formed part of the gardens of the old Brodsworth Hall and provided building stone for the eighteenth-century house. Quarry gardens were popular in the late eighteenth and early nineteenth centuries

as a means of incorporating a wild and Picturesque flavour into gardens. Perhaps the most highly developed quarry garden of that period is at Belsay Hall, Northumberland (also in the care of English Heritage). At Brodsworth the quarry is less dramatic, and its rocky dells and hollows were planted with more fussy civilised arrangements consonant with the period. This part of the garden had become seriously overgrown prior to its acquisition by English Heritage and is currently the subject of extensive replanting.

The Grove was a 'fairyland' of intersecting paths, banks and bridges, each separating the various internal vistas and areas of contrasting planting. Its first major feature is a rock garden, originally with a cascade of water flowing through a series of stone troughs into a drain. The bottom of the garden was covered with fine granite clippings to give the impression of a continuous flow of water. When restoration work is complete it will be possible to walk through the rock garden and up over the bridge to the summerhouse, from where there are fine views over the gardens.

The floor of the quarry is known as the Target Range, a long open space once flanked by formal iris borders, where the family and their friends could practise archery. At the south end is an 'eyecatcher' in the form of a façade of a small building built into the quarry wall. Dating from the 1860s, it was probably constructed with stone from the old hall. At the north end is the Target House. This curious building dates from the eighteenth century but was reroofed in a rustic Swiss chalet style in the 1860s. It now houses an exhibition devoted to the history of the gardens.

Rising from the floor of the quarry are two substantial artificial mounds now known as the spine banks, constructed of spoil from the quarry floor. Their purpose is to create a varied landscape within this otherwise confined section

of the garden. Recently replanted with specimen trees and shrubs, these banks were a favourite device of Victorian gardeners. At the north end of the Grove is the rose garden, set out on either side of a long, curved wrought-iron pergola. Early rose varieties have been planted within clipped box hedges to recreate the subtly coloured garden of the nineteenth century.

The lawns at Brodsworth have been left for many years without close cutting and the use of herbicides. As a consequence they are notably rich in wild flora, such as milkwort, rock rose, cowslips, rest-harrow and orchids – and, in early spring, narcissi – providing the Doncaster area with one of the few remaining areas of natural magnesian limestone grassland. Every attempt is being made to combine the reestablishment of this important example of an historic garden with the conservation of the site's rich natural history.

Since Brodsworth Hall and Gardens came into the care of English Heritage in 1990, a great deal of restoration and recovery work has been carried out in the gardens. The formal borders around the lawns have been cleared of under- and overgrowth, trees reshaped, and the shrubberies, flower and rose gardens replanted. Further plans include the reintroduction of nineteenth-century varieties of bedding plants and bulbs, and the reinstatement of the balustrade on the summerhouse, together with repair work on the paths between the summerhouse and rock garden. The rejuvenation of the gardens will continue well into the early twenty-first century.

The Target House, of eighteenth-century origin but thatched in Victorian times. It stands at the north end of the main quarry vista

LEFT *The bridge over the rock garden in the Grove. The stonework has been restored*

The rose garden, with its restored wrought-iron pergola, contains over 100 early rose varieties

Removing the unstable terracotta balustrade during roof repairs in 1993

When English Heritage acquired Brodsworth in April 1990, it faced a daunting prospect. The fabric of the building, as well as its interior decoration and contents and the gardens, had suffered from years of inadequate maintenance. A growing understanding of the problems facing the site led to the development of slightly different policies for the treatment and presentation of each of these elements. The need for the building to be made wind and watertight, for example, resulted in substantial renovations, while in the gardens the need to replant and rejuvenate has allowed the recovery of some original features. Inside the house it was decided that the fragile interiors could be conserved with as little restoration as possible.

The building fabric

Initial surveys revealed that water had come through the roof of the house, damaging virtually all the first-floor ceilings and even some of those on the ground floor. The causes were

Cleaning the stonework in 1993. The columns of the porte cochère had to be entirely replaced, as their corroding iron cores had caused the stone to fall off

twofold: nearby mining subsidence had caused the building to tilt, so that the intended falls in gutters and flat roofs were no longer effective; and in heavy snowfall the rainwater outlets had failed to cope with large quantities of water from snow that had built up on the roof. To correct these problems, the roofs have been completely stripped, adequate falls introduced, and the whole area re-covered with new slates and leads. An elaborate network of heating elements, activated by low temperatures, has been installed in the rainwater outlets.

A second major problem was the erosion of the magnesian limestone cladding of the building by acid rain. The decay was so severe that birds had been nesting for years in holes eroded through the stone of the porte cochère and around windows. The damage has now been repaired by replacing extensive areas of stone and careful cleaning to remove harmful pollution deposits.

The building had also been severely affected by rising damp, resulting in a band of erosion about 1m (3ft) high around the whole of the exterior, and causing paint and wallpaper to peel inside. Again, the cause of the damp has been identified and corrected, and much of the affected stonework has been replaced.

Repairs to the fabric of the building were essential not just for their own sake but so as to create the high standards of environmental control necessary for the long-term preservation of the interiors and contents. To maintain the required levels of temperature and humidity, all the services – water, central heating and electricity – have been renewed and upgraded. Doors and windows have been repaired and overhauled to eliminate draughts, and extensive measures taken to reduce the risk of fire.

Interior decoration and contents

Brodsworth's structural problems, particularly the damp, led to considerable damage in the interiors; there were widespread losses to the plasterwork, painted marbling and wallpapers. The fluctuating temperature and humidity had made the delicate surfaces such as the wall

paint, gilding and oil paintings flake badly, and had warped and cracked furniture. The subsidence had made almost every fireplace unstable and had resulted in cracks in the plasterwork and painted glass window. Exposure to sunlight, together with general wear and tear, caused all the wall silks, upholstery and carpets to fade and start to disintegrate. The accumulation of dust and dirt provided ideal conditions for insect pest infestation to take hold; textiles, carpets and furniture were badly affected by moth, carpet beetle and woodworm. Almost everything was in an extremely fragile condition.

It gradually became understood, through conservation surveys, cataloguing the collections and researching the history of the house and family, that some of these were longstanding problems. There had been regular touching up of paintwork, reupholstery, and replacement of curtains and carpets throughout the history of the house. However, the extent of the damage found in 1990 had been exacerbated in later years by the dwindling number of staff, lack of maintenance and changes in the use of the house, such as the gradual withdrawal of the Grant-Daltons from some rooms on the first floor and the Servants' Wing.

This raised many issues about the conservation and presentation of Brodsworth: it is important as an example of a house built and furnished in the 1860s, but the original appearance of the interiors had been much altered over the years. Their perilous condition was a result of, and inextricably intertwined with, the later history of the house and family. Eventually it was decided not to attempt to restore the interiors to the 1860s, but to preserve as far as possible the surviving contents and evidence of change so as to tell the entire history of the house. This is perhaps part of a wider move away from the policy of restoring

historic houses to one particular period, together with a growing interest in their changing fortunes and a greater acceptance of decay.

The general aim was to slow down the decay and to stabilise the objects and decoration as far as possible as they had been found, keeping the overall atmosphere of decline. Following the principles of museum conservation, all treatments are, where possible, reversible, so that the work can be altered or taken further in future. In practice this involved widespread but gentle cleaning, to remove the harmful dirt which could also harbour pests. Although this approach was applied consistently, in an attempt to maintain the visual balance of the whole house, it did have a different effect on certain features. For example, the varnished marbling could be washed fairly easily, revealing something of the vibrancy and contrasts of the original (albeit faded) scheme, while wallpapers and silks could only be gently brushed or vacuumed.

In addition to the condition surveys, a computer-based inventory of the contents showed that Brodsworth contained no fewer than 17,000 objects, ranging from oil paintings and sculptures to household linen and kitchen implements, dating from the 1860s to the 1980s. The policy of conserving and displaying the entire history of the house means that, for example, modern basins and electric fires have been retained in addition to the Victorian washstands and fireplaces.

LEFT *Damage to the plaster decoration and silk wall hangings in the Drawing Rooms, caused by a leaking downpipe*

Paint conservation and plaster repairs in the Entrance Hall in 1993. Removing the dirt revealed both the colours of the earlier marbled paintwork and previous repairs

Flaking gilding had to be consolidated on site before the fragile gilt furniture could be transported

RIGHT *A pair of paintings by William Perry receiving conservation. Blackberrying, on the left, has had flaking paint secured and surface dirt removed while leaving the original varnish intact*

A pair of Lapworths' crimson curtains being conserved in 1992. The delicate silk braid is being removed before the curtain on the right is dry cleaned; it has been repositioned on the left curtain after cleaning

All the contents had to be taken into storage so that the repairs to the fabric of the building could take place. The decoration and fittings were also conserved by specialists while the house was empty. Wallpapers and silks were removed and conserved where necessary, or were given 'first aid' on the walls. Marbled paintwork was gently cleaned with soap and water, and all the flakes consolidated with adhesive. The damaged areas were simply touched in and the old repairs kept. Insect infestation was a major problem, and had caused considerable damage, especially to carpets and textiles. Urgent treatment was required, and a technique was employed which had been pioneered by the Victoria and Albert Museum. This involved deep-freezing textiles and carpets in an industrial freezer to kill the insects. The more complex objects such as furniture or stuffed birds were fumigated.

While the contents were in storage a rolling programme of conservation was started, which will take some years to complete. The textiles and carpets, being so fragile and such a huge part of the collection, have taken up much of the programme to date. Those now on display have been cleaned by vacuuming or washing, and then damaged areas have been supported or stitched. Almost invisible nylon net has been used to hold many of the fragile surfaces in place. Many still await conservation in store.

The furniture has received structural repairs and been lightly wax-polished. Most other types of object, such as the sculpture and ceramics, have been gently cleaned. Care was taken not to overpolish the metalwork in the Kitchen, so as

to maintain its character as a long-abandoned room. The oil paintings have been surface-cleaned and secured in their frames. More cosmetic work such as the removal of overpaint or revarnishing will be considered once the visual balance of the whole house and each room has been reassessed.

Great care has been taken in redisplaying the house to protect the decoration and contents as much as possible. Harmful ultra-violet light has been cut out by film on the windows, and daylight reduced by renewing the white holland blinds. Historic carpets are protected by over-laying druggets or carpet strips, although in the main circulation spaces accurate reproductions have replaced the originals, which were too worn to be reused.

All the work on the decoration and contents leading up to the opening of Brodsworth to the public aimed at making everything reasonably clean and stable, whilst retaining the appearance of a well-worn and currently well-cared for country house. In spite of the conservation and protective measures the interiors remain very fragile and easily damaged. High standards of housekeeping and continuing conservation are required, including monitoring to prevent insect infestation taking hold again. Although the major rooms and furnishings were redisplayed, many objects are still in store, in particular textiles such as the curtains from the Morning Room and bedrooms. It is hoped to continue steadily to conserve some of these to complete the display of rooms already open, and to refurnish at least two of the remaining west bedrooms.